ADVENT and CHRISTMAS
—— with ——
FULTON J. SHEEN

Advent and Christmas

with

Fulton J. Sheen

*Compiled and Edited
by Judy Bauer*

Liguori

Published by Liguori Publications
Liguori, Missouri
www.liguori.org

Scripture quotations are from the *New Revised Standard Version of the Bible*, copyright 1989 by the Division of Christian Education of the National Council of the Churches of Christ in the USA. Used by permission. All rights reserved.

This edition published in cooperation with the Society for the Propagation of the Faith, New York, New York.

Compliant with *The Roman Missal*, third edition.

Library of Congress Cataloging-in-Publication Data

Sheen, Fulton J. (Fulton John), 1895–1979.
    Advent and Christmas with Fulton J. Sheen / compiled and edited by Judy Bauer.
       p. cm.
    Includes bibliographical references.
    ISBN 978-0-7648-0749-7 (pbk.)
    1. Advent—Prayer-books and devotions—English. 2. Christmas—Prayer-books and devotions—English. 3. Epiphany—Prayer-books and devotions—English. 4. Catholic Church—Prayer-books and devotions—English. I. Bauer, Judy, 1941– II. Title.

BX2170.A4 S54 2001
242'.33—dc21   2001029390

Printed in the United States of America
19 18 17 16 15 / 11 10 9 8 7

Contents

*J*ohn of the Cross, in his book *The Living Flame of Love*, compares our pre-Advent selves to green logs that have been thrown into a fire, the fire of love. Green logs, we know, do not immediately burst into flame. Rather, being young and full of moisture, they sizzle for a long time before they reach kindling temperature and can take into themselves the fire that is around them.

So, too, the rhythm of love. Only the really mature can truly burst into flame within community. The rest of us are still too self-contained, too green, too selfish, too damp....What helps change this is precisely the tension in our lives. In carrying tension, we come to kindling temperature and are made ready for love....

The sublime has to be waited for. Only when there is first enough heat will there be unity. To give birth to what's divine requires the slow patience of gestation. In shorthand, that's the algebra of Advent.

RONALD ROLHEISER, OMI

Introduction

"PEACE BE WITH YOU." These are Bishop Fulton J. Sheen's familiar opening words to many of his television and radio broadcasts. For Bishop Sheen, the concept of inner peace was a central one to his approach to spreading God's Word. The following quotation sums up Bishop Sheen's message about peace:

> Inner peace can be won only by making God the ruler of all that we do. Many people who believe in God refuse to go this far: they keep Him in a small compartment of their minds. Their plans are laid without consulting Him; their trials and sufferings are endured…and their days are passed in loneliness and weariness, although each hour might have been filled with sweetness.
>
> To such hearts a single moment of grace may work the change. They suddenly become aware that "the Lord is in the house." Better still, the Lord is in our hearts. They are no longer self-centered, now, but they are God-centered; outer events of their lives can no longer ruffle their peace.

This concern for the salvation of the individual—the possession of the true peace of Christ—is a theme that runs through Bishop Sheen's entire ministry from his boyhood in Peoria, Illinois, to his days as a student for the priesthood, to his theological training at the University of Louvain in Belgium and to his work as a widely loved radio and TV personality.

True to Sheen's vision, this companion through Advent and Christmas can be seen as a personal journey of transformation from the self-centered to the God-centered, from green logs to kindling, from outer chaos to inner peace—the same peace witnessed to by the angels of Bethlehem.

How to Use This Book

ADVENT—that period of great anticipatory joy—is a time of preparation for the celebration of Christ's arrival in Bethlehem as a helpless infant. In the Western liturgy, Advent begins four Sundays prior to December 25—the Sunday closest to November 30 which is the feast of Saint Andrew, one of Jesus' first disciples. The annual commemoration of Christ's birth begins the Christmas cycle of the liturgical year—a cycle which runs from Christmas Eve to the Sunday after the feast of the Epiphany. In keeping with the unfolding of the message of the liturgical year, this book is designed to be used during the entire period from the first Sunday of Advent to the end of the Christmas cycle. The four weeks of Advent are often thought of as symbolizing the four different ways that Christ comes into the world: (1) at his birth as a helpless infant at Bethlehem; (2) at his arrival in the hearts of believers; (3) at his death; and (4) at his arrival on Judgment Day.

Because Christmas falls on a different day of the week each year, the fourth week of Advent is never really finished; it is abruptly, joyously, and solemnly abrogated by the annual coming again of Christ at Christmas. Christ's Second Coming will also one day abruptly interrupt our sojourn here on earth.

Since the calendar dictates the number of days in Advent, this book includes Scripture and meditation readings for a full twenty-eight days. These twenty-eight daily readings make up Part I of this book. It is suggested that the reader begin at the beginning and then on Christmas Day switch to Part II, which contains materials for the twelve days of Christmas. If there are any "extra" entries from Part I, these may be read by doubling up days, if so desired, or by reading two entries on weekends. Alternately, one may just skip those entries that do not fit within the Advent time frame for that particular year.

Part III of this book proposes two optional formats for using each daily entry as part of a longer liturgical observance similar to Night Prayer combined with a version of the Office of Readings. These options are for those who may wish to use this book as part of a more-developed individual or group observance.

The purpose of these readings is to enrich the Advent/Christmas/Epiphany season of the liturgical year and set up a means by which individuals, families, or groups may observe the true meaning of the season.

PART I

~~~~~~

READINGS for ADVENT

DAY 1

[T]hose who wait for the LORD
shall renew their strength,
they shall mount up with wings
like eagles,
they shall run and not be weary,
they shall walk and not faint.

ISAIAH 40:31

Waiting in Silence

*G*od walks into your soul with silent step. God comes to you more than you go to Him. Never will his coming be what you expect, and yet never will it disappoint. The more you respond to his gentle pressure, the greater will be your freedom.

Simple Truths

❖ ❖ ❖

Restore, O God, my sight, unclose my lips, and open my soul, so that when your gracious Word is sent, I will be able to shout joyfully to you, "Come." Let the longing of this season of Advent transmute into a proper preparation for the arrival of the World's Greatest Love. Let my green self be matured and transformed into a living flame of love.

DAY 2

For a child has been born for us,
a son given to us;
authority rests upon his shoulders;
and he is named
Wonderful Counselor, Mighty God,
Everlasting Father,
Prince of Peace.

ISAIAH 9:6

Timeless Opportunities

*T*ime opens opportunities. When Moses led his people out of Egypt, God spoke to him: "You have been going about this mountain country long enough: turn northward." The time of probation was paid; the time of opportunity had come. The emancipation of the slaves waited for Lincoln; the open door of Ephesus for Paul....

Though time is too precious to waste, it must never be thought that what was lost is irretrievable. Once the Divine is introduced, then comes the opportunity to make up for losses. God is the God of the second chance. Peter denied, but he had the second chance in which to become as solid as a rock. Jonah, who refused to accept a mission, was given a second chance and saved Babylon. There really is such a thing as a "second birth." Being born again means that all that went before is not held against us.

ON BEING HUMAN

❖ ❖ ❖

Welcome, little infant of the world, you who were God-sent to us more than two thousand years ago. Let your birth give us a fresh heart and time for second chances. Let your birth retrieve for us the opportunity to repair our sinful selves.

DAY 3

But you, O Bethlehem of Ephrathah,
who are one of the little clans of Judah,
from you shall come forth for me
one who is to rule in Israel,
whose origin is from of old,
from ancient days.

MICAH 5:2

Two Births, Two Bethlehems

*T*here are two births of Christ, one unto the world in Bethlehem; the other in the soul, when it is spiritually reborn. Men think of the former much more than the later, and celebrate it every year; but the spiritual Bethlehem is equally momentous....

It was the second birth that Saint Paul insisted on when he wrote from prison to his beloved people, the Ephesians, asking that Christ may dwell in their hearts by faith and that they be rooted and grounded in love. This is the second Bethlehem, or the personal relationship of the individual heart to the Lord Christ.

REJOICE

Jesus, may I be just as willing and determined to follow the road of the second Bethlehem, as Mary and Joseph were to set off on their journey to the first Bethlehem. Let me recognize that Advent is not just a sentimental exercise but a true journey of conversion. May this Advent occasion your rebirth and rootedness in my heart in both faith and love.

DAY 4

A shoot shall come out from the stump of Jesse,
and a branch shall grow out of his roots.
The spirit of the LORD shall rest on him,
the spirit of wisdom and understanding,
the spirit of counsel and might,
the spirit of knowledge and the
fear of the LORD....
The wolf shall live with the lamb,
the leopard shall lie down with the kid,
the calf and the lion and the
fatling together,
and a little child shall lead them.

ISAIAH 11:1–2, 6

Death Before Life

*T*he story of every human life begins with birth and ends with death. In the person of Christ, however, it was his death that was first and his life that was last. The Scripture describes him as "the Lamb slain as it were, from the beginning of the world." He was slain in intention by the first sin and rebellion against God. It was not so much that his birth cast a shadow on his life and thus led to his death; it was rather that the Cross was first, and cast its shadow back to his birth. His has been the only life in the world that was ever lived backward...from the reason of his coming manifested by his name "Jesus" or "Savior" to the fulfillment of his coming, namely, his death on the Cross.

LIFE OF CHRIST

You, O Lord, are the one whose coming was foretold. We long for your birth which is newly dear each year. Let your birth find us blessed with the spirit of peace and understanding, and find the lion and the lamb in the same lair. Let the Crib and the Cross be our autobiography as well. Let these be the two symbols that shadow our lives as disciples here on earth.

DAY 5

"Give and it will be given to you.
A good measure, pressed down,
shaken together, running over,
will be put into your lap;
for the measure you give
will be the measure you get back."

LUKE 6:38

Gifts and Justice

*Y*ou might say that it was very unjust of God to deprive us of friendship with him, and of these other gifts, simply because Adam sinned. There would have been injustice if God deprived you of your due, but you are no more entitled to be a child of God than a razor has a right to bloom, or a rose has the right to bark, or a dog has the right to quote Dante. What Adam lost was gifts, not a heritage.

On Christmas Day, when you distribute gifts to your friends, would I have a right to say to you: "Why do you not give me a gift?" You would answer: "I am not doing you an injustice, because I owe you nothing. I am not obliged to give these gifts to my friends. If I had not given them gifts, I would not have deprived them of anything I owed them." So, neither did God owe us anything beyond our nature as a creature of his handiwork.

PREFACE TO RELIGION

❖ ❖ ❖

Lord, as I gather my offerings in thanksgiving for the gift of your Beloved Son, let me remember the needs of those for whom my gifts are an obligatory duty, not an act of mere generosity. Grant me the grace to give to those in need always, not just during this season of the year. Above all, inspire me to give in the fullest possible measure.

DAY 6

*The wisdom of the humble lifts
their heads high,
and seats them among the great.
Do not praise individuals
for their good looks,
or loathe anyone
because of appearance alone.
The bee is small among flying creatures,
but what it produces is the best
of sweet things.
Do not boast about wearing fine clothes,
and do not exalt yourself when
you are honored;
for the words of the Lord are wonderful....*

SIRACH 11:1–4

Big to Little

*T*here is a close relation between physical littleness, which is childhood, and mental littleness, which is humility. We cannot always be children, which is another way of saying we can be humble. And so in the spiritual order the law remains ever the same: if human beings are ever to discover anything big, they must always be making themselves little; if they magnify their ego to the infinite, they will discover nothing, for there is nothing bigger than the infinite; but if they reduce their ego to zero, then they will discover everything big—for there is nothing smaller than the self. How, then, shall we find the reason behind the joy? Just as it is only by being little that we discover anything big, so it is only by being humble that we will find an Infinite God in the form of a little child.

Eternal Galilean

Lord, our God, help us to prepare for the coming of your Son by seeking the small rather than the large, humility instead of honors, good works instead of good looks. Help us to see that your coming is the reason behind the joy—the God behind the child.

DAY 7

Let us love one another,
because love is from God;
everyone who loves is born of God
and knows God....
The commandment we have from him is this:
those who love God
must love their brothers and sisters also.

1 JOHN 4:7, 21

Love's Mystery

O nce I surrender the tinsel to have the jewel, then I enter into the mystery of love. I see that I do not love anyone unless he has some goodness in him, or is lovable in some way. But, I see also that God did not love me because I am lovable. I became lovable because God poured some of his goodness and love into me. I then began to apply this charity to my neighbor. If I do not find him lovable, I have to put love into him as God puts love into me, and thereby I provoke the response of love. Now, my personality is restored and I make the great discovery that no one is happy until he loves both God and neighbor.

SIMPLE TRUTHS

✤ ✤ ✤

Grant, O Lord, that I may ignore the tinsel and the dazzle of this season and, in anticipation and hope, keep my eyes fixed on you, the precious jewel of my life. Grant me growth in your gift of goodness and give me eyes to truly see the lovability of all those I encounter.

DAY 8

Therefore the Lord himself
will give you a sign.
Look, the young woman is with child
and shall bear a son,
and shall name him Immanuel.
He shall eat curds and honey
by the time he knows how
to refuse the evil and choose the good.

ISAIAH 7:14–15

Mother of Mothers

ecause [Mary] is what God wanted us all to be, she speaks of herself as the eternal blueprint in the mind of God, the one whom God loved before she was a creature. She is even pictured as being with Him not only at creation, but before creation. She existed in the Divine Mind as an Eternal Thought before there were any mothers. She is the Mother of mothers. The closer one is to God, the greater the purity. But since no one was ever closer to God than the woman whose human portals he threw open to walk this earth, then no one could have been more pure than she.

This special purity of hers we call the Immaculate Conception. The word "immaculate" is taken from two Latin words meaning "not stained." "Conception" means that, at the first moment of her conception, the Blessed Mother in the womb of her mother, Saint Anne, and in virtue of the anticipated merits of the Redemption of her Son was preserved free from the stains of original sin.

❖ ❖ ❖   THE WORLD'S FIRST LOVE

O Lord and Everlasting God, you who came down to earth as the Greatest of All Gifts, help me to achieve a clean heart so that I may grow in closeness to you and your Mother. Let this dance of waiting remind us that we are a people whose call is to bring forth Christ in the stillness of our hearts—as Mary brought forth her Son in the wintry stillness of the cave in Bethlehem.

DAY 9

"Come, let us go up to the
mountain of the LORD,
to the house of the God of Jacob;
that he may teach us his ways
and that we may walk in his paths."
…He shall judge between the nations,
and shall arbitrate for many peoples;
they shall beat their swords into plowshares,
and their spears into pruning hooks;
nation shall not lift up sword
against nation,
neither shall they learn war any more.

ISAIAH 2:3–4

The Message of Christmas

The Christmas message is not that peace will come automatically, because Christ is born in Bethlehem; that birth in Bethlehem was the prelude to His birth in our hearts by grace and faith and love. Peace belongs only to those who will to have it. If there is no peace in the world today, it is not because Christ did not come; it is because we did not let Him in.

SIMPLE TRUTHS

✤ ✤ ✤

Heavenly Father, I thank you for the most gracious gift of your Son, our Divine Savior. We offer to you our prayers of thanksgiving for all the many blessings you have bestowed on us—now and always. Enfold us daily in your peace that passes all understanding. Let us all rejoice in the Lord for He is coming. Help us live our invitation to the Babe by the worthiness of our daily actions.

DAY 10

*"Let the light of your face shine
on us, O LORD!"
You have put gladness in my heart
more than when their grain and
wine abound.
I will both lie down and sleep in peace;
for you alone, O LORD,
make me lie down in safety.*

PSALM 4:6–8

Truth and Light

*C*hrist's coming into the world was not like that of a sightseer to a strange city, but rather like that of an artist visiting his own studio, or an author paging the books he himself has written, for in becoming incarnate the Divine Word was tabernacling himself in his own creation. His human nature in no way limited his Divine Wisdom, but it did give him a new way of communicating it to humans, and one quite comfortable to their own nature. Through a human tongue like their own, speaking their own dialect, people hear him say, "I am the light of the world...."

IN THE FULLNESS OF TIME

Remind me often during this Advent season, O Lord Jesus, that you are the light that shines in the darkness. Have mercy on us, your children, and aid us in following the path of your light so that we may not perish but reach eternal life. As we are claimed by the outer signs of this season—the gifts, the family gatherings, the tree, the lights, and the decorations—let us discover in them the hope and faith of your coming—which is the true "magic of Christmas."

DAY 11

For old age is not honored
for length of time,
or measured by number of years;
but understanding is gray hair for anyone,
and a blameless life is ripe old age....
Being perfected in a short time,
they fulfilled long years;
for their souls were pleasing to the Lord,
therefore he took them quickly....

WISDOM 4:8–9, 13–14

The Coronation of Childhood

here is no escape from the tremendous fact of Christmas day, that when God revealed himself to this poor world of ours, men cried in astonishment: "Why, it is a child?" And so it is that the closer we get to God the more we become children, and the closer God gets to us the more he becomes a child. No one in the world ever suspected that the Ancient of Days who presided at creation would take his throne in that creation as a babe in a crib, just as no one ever thought he would tell the old men of forty, like Nicodemus, that they must be born again.

According to all worldly standards, it is the aged who are learned. And yet when Wisdom came to earth he was a child, and when Wise Men came to Wisdom they were told to be like children. Christmas, then, is the coronation of childhood, the glorification of the young whose hearts are simple, the proclamation to aging hearts that the world need not despair and die, because the Fountain of Youth has come into it to...turn time backward, make old things young again.

In the Fullness of Time

✦ ✦ ✦

Lord, you who humbled yourself to come as a little Child to live in our sinful world, help us to grow in simplicity and love—those qualities shown by the first shepherds of your birth. Keep us close to your crib and help us praise the Babe whose coming teaches us to love and live. Make fruitful this Advent time of inner preparation so that with the carol we may sing "Let every heart prepare Him room."

DAY 12

The angel [Gabriel] said to her, "Do not be afraid, Mary, for you have found favor with God. And now, you will conceive in your womb and bear a son, and you will name him Jesus. He will be great, and will be called the Son of the Most High, and the Lord God will give to him the throne of his ancestor David. He will reign over the house of Jacob forever, and of his kingdom there will be no end." Mary said to the angel, "How shall this be, since I am a virgin?"

LUKE 1:30–34

The Great Birth Announcement

*O*ur Blessed Mother…said "I know not man." Why is there a value in not knowing man? Because she had consecrated her virginity to God. At a moment when every woman sought the privilege of being the Mother of the Messiah, Mary gave up hope and received it….

If the condition of becoming the Mother of God was the surrender of her vow, she would not make that surrender, knowing man would have been evil for her, though it would not have been evil in other circumstances. Not knowing man is a kind of ignorance, but here it proves to be such a blessing that in an instant the Holy Spirit overshadows her, making her a living ciborium privileged to bear within herself for nine months the Guest who is the Host of the world.

THE SEVEN WORDS OF JESUS AND MARY

Holy Child, our Redeemer, free us from our disordered trust in our own knowledge, will, and abilities. Award us courage to follow your will as most perfectly expressed in your most Holy Mother Immaculate. May we use this preparation time to learn to love You ever more deeply, displacing our sinful ignorance so that we may be your manger and ciborium in this world today.

DAY 13

Mary set out and went with haste to a Judean town in the hill country, where she entered the house of Zechariah and greeted Elizabeth. When Elizabeth heard Mary's greeting, the child leaped in her womb. And Elizabeth was filled with the Holy Spirit and exclaimed with a loud cry..."Blessed is she who believed that there would be a fulfillment of what was spoken to her by the Lord."

LUKE 1:39–45

Fulfillment of God's Will

In what does your life consist except two things: (1) Active duties; and (2) passive circumstances. The first is under your control; do these in God's name. The second is outside your control; these submit to in God's name. Consider only the present; leave the past to God's justice, the future to his Providence. Perfection of personality does not consist in knowing God's plan, but in submitting to it as it reveals itself in the circumstances of life.

There is really one shortcut to sanctity—the one Mary chose in the Visitation, the one Our Lord chose in Gethsemane—abandonment to the Divine Will.

THE SEVEN WORDS OF JESUS AND MARY

✣ ✣ ✣

O God, our Savior, let me rejoice in your favor; fill me with the good things of your Holy Spirit, as the unborn infant Jesus filled the womb of Mary. Give me the courage to do all things in God's name—those that I actively control and those to which I must patiently submit—and give me the grace to know the difference.

DAY 14

When his mother Mary had been engaged to Joseph, but before they had lived together, she was found to be with child from the Holy Spirit. Her husband Joseph, being a righteous man and unwilling to expose her to public disgrace, planned to dismiss her quietly. But just when he had resolved to do this, an angel of the Lord appeared to him in a dream and said, "Joseph, son of David, do not be afraid to take Mary as your wife, for the child conceived in her is from the Holy Spirit. She will bear a son, and you are to name him Jesus, for he will save his people from their sins."

MATTHEW 1:18–21

Blessed Be His Name

*E*very babe ever born to this life, except One, was born to live. The only exception was the Babe who gave Christmas its name. The name given to Him at his birth was "Jesus" because, as the angels said, "He shall save his people from their sins." He took not the name of "Teacher," for then he would have been only an ethical reformer; nor did he take the name of "Judge," for that would be to announce judgment before announcing mercy and forgiveness. Later on, when he begins his public life, John salutes him as the "Lamb who takes away the sins of the world."

Arnold Toynbee speaks of three would-be saviors—the savior who believes in automatic progress; the savior with the sword who cannot sheathe it when he has cut his way to the throne; and the savior who tries to save the world with philosophical sayings. None of these, says Toynbee, can bring salvation; the only one who can save civilization is the Savior who saves us from our sins. Pointing to Christ he says, "There is the Savior." Yes, and there is Christmas—a Babe wrapped in swaddling clothes.

THOUGHTS FOR DAILY LIVING

✢ ✢ ✢

Christ, our High Priest and Savior, give us the wisdom and perseverance to combat temptation and to overcome sin so that we may, with clean robes and clean hearts, find salvation and follow the "river of death into everlasting life." Especially during this holy time of your birthday in Bethlehem, help us to love and forgive, to cope with the hectic pressures of the season, and grant us patience to deal graciously with all that we encounter.

DAY 15

This is the testimony given by John [the Baptist] when the Jews sent priests and Levites from Jerusalem to ask…"Who are you?" …He said, / "I am the voice of one crying out in the wilderness, / 'Make straight the way of the Lord,'" / as the prophet Isaiah said.

Now they…asked him, "Why then are you baptizing if you are neither the Messiah, nor Elijah, nor the prophet?"

John answered them, "I baptize with water. Among you stands one whom you do not know, the one who is coming after me; I am not worthy to untie the thong of his sandal."

JOHN 1:19–27

The Precursor

*T*he world's greatest need is someone who will understand that there is no greater conquest than victory over oneself; someone who will realize that real worth is achieved not so much by activity, as by silence, …who will, like a lightning flash, burn away the bonds of feeble interest which tie down our energies to the world; who with a fearless voice, like John the Baptist, will arouse our enfeebled nature out of the sleek dream of unheroic response; someone who will gain victories not by stepping down from the Cross and compromising with the world, but who will suffer in order to conquer the world.

MOODS AND TRUTHS

✤ ✤ ✤

Lord God, let us, like John the Baptist, be persons of retirement, given to penance and self-denial. Let us prepare your way in our own hearts and let us be unwaveringly faithful to you whether we are praised or ridiculed, whether we prosper in this world or fail, whether we are sick or well, and whether we suffer or are happy. May we be your precursors as you once again reach across time and eternity to break into our waiting world.

DAY 16

His divine power has given us everything needed for life and godliness, through the knowledge of him who called us by his own glory and goodness. Thus he has given us, through these things, his precious and very great promises, so that through them you may escape from the corruption that is in the world...and may become participants of the divine nature.

2 PETER 1:3–4

Divine Yet Human

*N*o person can love anything unless he can get his arms around it....But once God became a babe and was wrapped in swaddling clothes and laid in a manger, men could say, "This is Emmanuel, this is God with us." By his reaching down to frail human nature and lifting it up to the incomparable prerogative of union with himself, human nature became dignified. So real was this union that all of his acts and words, all of his agonies and tears, all of his thoughts and reasonings, resolves and emotions, while being properly human, were at the same time the acts and words, agonies and tears, thoughts and reasons, resolves and emotions, of the Eternal Son of God.

LIFE OF CHRIST

✤ ✤ ✤

Lord God, Heavenly Father, Almighty Creator of the universe, we thank you for sending us the gift of your dearly beloved Son in the form of a new-born Babe—a human yet divine being. Allow us the further gift of knowing and loving you, of getting our arms locked securely around the God-With-Us. May this embrace be our safety net in our struggle for eternal life.

DAY 17

God's foolishness is wiser than human wisdom, and God's weakness is stronger than human strength....But God chose what is foolish in the world to shame the wise; God chose what is weak in the world to shame the strong; God chose what is low and despised in the world, things that are not, to reduce to nothing things that are, so that no one might boast in the presence of God. He is the source of your life in Christ Jesus, who became for us wisdom from God, and righteousness and sanctification and redemption.

1 CORINTHIANS 1:25–30

Human Foolishness

*T*here are several ways to avoid loving God:

Deny that you are a sinner.

Pretend that religion is for the ignorant and the superstitious, but not for the truly learned such as yourself.

Insist that the sole purpose of religion is social service.

Judge religion by whether or not it is accepted by the "important" people of the world.

Avoid all contemplation, self-examination, and inquiry into the moral state of your soul.

GOD LOVE YOU

✣ ✣ ✣

O Wisdom of the Most High, who orders all things from beginning to end, teach us to act and speak according to the standards set by Jesus Christ. Give us awareness of the things that are to come and a taste for the eternal and divine. Let us see our sins with clarity, let us wholeheartedly accept our Faith as the road to salvation. Let us examine the moral state of our soul with a fearless eye and, finally, let us pray always with a passionate heart.

DAY 18

*"Whoever is faithful
in a very little is faithful
also in much."*

LUKE 16:10

*One who despises small things
will fail little by little.*

SIRACH 19:1

The Message of the Swaddling Clothes

*T*he swaddling clothes of an infant hid the Son of God in Bethlehem, and the appearance of bread and wine hides the Reality of Christ dying again on Calvary, in the Mass. This concealment of Himself that God effects with us is operative in his use of the Now to hide his will beneath the aspect of very simple, everyday things. We live our lives in dependence on such casual, common benefits as air and water; so Our Lord is pleased to receive from us in return the thousands of unimportant actions and the trifling details that make up our lives—provided that we see, even in our sorrows, "The shade of his hand outstretched caressingly." Here is the whole secret of sanctity; the method is available to everyone and deserves particular notice from those who ask: "What can I do?" For many good souls are hungry to do great things for God. They complain that they have no opportunities for heroic virtue, no chance at the apostolate. They would be martyrs; but when a meal is late, or a bus is crowded, when the theater is filled, or the dance postponed, or the bacon overdone, they are upset for a whole day. They miss their opportunities for loving God in the little things He asks of them.

LIFT UP YOUR HEART

✦ ✦ ✦

Dear Lord, during this season of Advent preparation, help us to look inward instead of being distracted by the outward. Give each of us the opportunity to search our conscience and seek your will—especially as you reveal it in the seemingly insignificant events of daily life. May our works dispel the darkness of our broken world until such time as Christ will come again.

DAY 19

In those days a decree went out from Emperor Augustus that all the world should be registered. ...All went to their own towns to be registered. Joseph also went from the town of Nazareth in Galilee to Judea, to the city of David called Bethlehem, because he was descended from the house and family of David. He went to be registered with Mary, to whom he was engaged and who was expecting a child....And she gave birth to her first-born son and wrapped him in bands of cloth, and laid him in a manger, because there was no place for them in the inn.

LUKE 2:1–7

No Room in the Inn

Mary is now with child, awaiting birth, and Joseph is full of expectancy as he enters the city of his own family. He searched for a place for the birth of him to whom heaven and earth belonged. Could it be that the Creator would not find room in his own creation?

Certainly, thought Joseph, there would be room in the village inn. There was room for the rich; there was room for those who were clothed in soft garments....But when finally the scrolls of history are completed down to the last word of time, the saddest lines of all will be: "There was no room in the inn." No room in the inn, but there was room in the stable. The inn was the gathering place of public opinion, the focal point of the world's moods, the rendezvous of the worldly, the rallying place of the popular and the successful. But there's no room in the place where the world gathers. The stable is a place for outcasts, the ignored, and the forgotten. The world might have expected the Son of God to be born in an inn; a stable would certainly be the last place in the world where one would look for him. The lesson is: divinity is always where you least expect to find it. So the Son of God-Made-Man is invited to enter into his own world through a back door.

BISHOP SHEEN CATECHISM

✤ ✤ ✤

Lord, open my vision so that I may see divinity in all the unexpected places. Overflow my heart with hospitality so that I may shelter the ignored and the forgotten. Give me the grace to share my good fortune with others, and thereby usher in the Christ Child through the front door.

DAY 20

For you know the generous act
of our Lord Jesus Christ,
that though he was rich,
yet for your sakes he became poor,
so that by his poverty
you might become rich.

2 CORINTHIANS 8:9

Rich and Poor

We must not make the sentimental mistake of thinking Our Lord was just a poor man. He was a rich person who became a poor man. Rich he was in his divine nature because he was God, and Lord of heaven and earth. And yet despite that richness he became poor, principally because he became man. That is poverty of the worst kind, because it is limitation.

He who was born poor in a stable could have been born rich in a palace by the Tiber. Roman legions might have guarded him at his birth, instead of an ox and an ass. No one would have expected that he who made the gold of Caesar's throne would be born on a bed of straw; nor that he who made the warmth of the sun would be warmed by the breath of oxen; nor that he who owned the earth would be homeless on the earth. It is no wonder then that the first to come to his crib were the rich Magi and the poor Shepherds. Two things happened to them—the rich lost their avarice, for they gave their wealth to the poor; the poor lost their envy, for they learned that there is another wealth than that which the rich give away.

LIBERTY, EQUALITY, AND FRATERNITY

❖ ❖ ❖

O coming Christ, O Good News of Great Joy, you who have called me by name and redeemed me, banish my fears and bring the reassurance of your presence. Comfort me in my wilderness of uncertainty, discouragement, and confusion. Let me always recognize that you—however disguised—have shattered the darkness of a captive world and let me give glory to God for the Savior that has been born to us.

DAY 21

In the time of King Herod, after Jesus was born in Bethlehem of Judea, wise men from the East came to Jerusalem, asking, "Where is the child who has been born king of the Jews? For we observed his star at its rising, and have come to pay him homage."

MATTHEW 2:1–3

"Take care that you do not despise one of these little ones; for, I tell you, in heaven their angels continually see the face of my Father in heaven....So it is not the will of your Father in heaven that one of these little ones should be lost."

MATTHEW 18:10, 14

Searching for the Christ Child

The Russian peasantry for centuries has propagated a curious tradition. It is about an old woman, the Baboushka, who was at work in her house when the wise men came from the East and passed on their way to Bethlehem to find the Child. "Come with us," they said. "We have seen his star in the East, and we go to worship him."

"I will come, but not now. I have much housework to do, and when that is finished, I will follow and find him." But her work was never done. And the Three Kings had passed on their way across the desert, and the star shone no more in the darkened heavens.

Baboushka never saw the Christ Child, but she is still living and searching for him. And though she did not find him, out of love for him, she takes care of all his children....The tradition has it that she believes that in each poor child whom she warms and feeds, she may find the Christ Child whom she neglected long ago. But she is not doomed to disappointment, for the Divine Child said, "He who receives one of these little ones in my name, receives me."

REJOICE

❖ ❖ ❖

Jesus, you who took the little children into your arms, let our hearts echo this welcome to all whom we meet. Let us heed your message of love and see the Holy Child in every person we encounter.

DAY 22

*Better is the end of a thing than its beginning;
the patient in spirit are better than the proud in spirit.*

ECCLESIASTES 7:8

*Those who are patient stay calm
until the right moment,
and then cheerfulness comes back to them.
They hold back their words until the right moment;
then the lips of many tell of their good sense.*

SIRACH 2:23–24

*Accept whatever befalls you,
and in times of humiliation be patient.
For gold is tested in the fire,
and those found acceptable,
in the furnace of humiliation.*

SIRACH 2:4–5

Patience and Waiting

*T*he Greek origin of the word patience suggests two ideas: one continuance, the other submission. Combined, they mean submissive waiting; a frame of mind which is willing to wait because it knows it thus serves God and his holy purposes. A person who believes in nothing beyond this world is very impatient, because he has only a limited time in which to satisfy his wants.

Patience is not something one is born with; it is something that is achieved. Sight is a gift of nature, but seeing has to be won. So it is with self-possession and patience; such a virtue is developed by resistance and control.

There are many who excuse themselves, saying that if they were in other circumstances they would be much more patient. It makes little difference where we are; it all depends on what we are thinking about. What happens to us is not so important, but rather how we react to what happens. Tribulation tries the soul, and in the strong it develops patience, and patience, in its turn, hope.

WAY TO INNER PEACE

❖ ❖ ❖

As we await your coming during this Advent, O Lord, help us to practice the patience of love. Let us graciously endure the wrongs of criticism—whether just or unjust. Help us to maintain our inner calm in the face of disappointments—whether rain on the day of the picnic or the raise in pay that never comes. Help us to calmly greet the provocations of daily life. Remind us that to lose our reasonableness is to aggravate the troubles we must endure and only postpones their solution.

DAY 23

For the grace of God has appeared,
bringing salvation to all, training us to…
live lives that are self-controlled,
upright, and godly,
while we wait for the blessed hope
and the manifestation of the glory
of our great God and Savior,
Jesus Christ.

TITUS 2:11–14

Divine Exchange

*S*anctity is not giving up the world. It is exchanging the world. It is a continuation of that sublime transaction of the Incarnation in which Christ said to man: "You give me your humanity, I will give you my divinity. You give me your time, I will give you my eternity. You give me your bonds, I will give you my omnipotence. You give me your slavery, I will give you my freedom. You give me your death, I will give you my life. You give me your nothingness, I will give you my all." And the consoling thought throughout this whole transforming process is that it does not require much time to make us saints; it requires only much love.

GO TO HEAVEN

✤ ✤ ✤

God of all Goodness, in this season of exchanging gifts, help us to grow in knowledge of your great generosity to us sinners. Your presence in the crib of Bethlehem is a witness to our own sorry need for your cure and care. Help us to lay our souls at your feet, and in exchange give us solace for our hearts and the consoling gift of your redemption.

DAY 24

"You are the light of the world. A city built on a hill cannot be hid. No one after lighting a lamp puts it under the bushel basket, but on a lampstand, and it gives light to all in the house. In the same way, let your light shine before others, so that they may see your good works and give glory to your Father in heaven."

MATTHEW 5:14–16

Discovering the Divine Light

*G*o back to that night when Divine Light, in order to illumine the darkness of men, tabernacled himself in the world he had made, and you will see that only the simple and the learned found him, namely, the shepherds and the wise men. The angels and a star caught up in the reflection of that Light, as a torch lighted by a torch, and passed it on to the watchers of sheep and the searchers of skies. And lo! as the shepherds watched their flocks about the hills of Bethlehem, they were shaken by the light of the angels....And lo! as wise men from beyond the land of Media and Persia searched the heavens, the brilliance of a star, like a tabernacle lamp in the sanctuary of God's creation, beckoned them on to the stable where the star seemed to lose its light in the unearthly brilliance of the Light of the World.

ETERNAL GALILEAN

Jesus, Divine Light, True Light of all the world, through your grace help me shine my light through the lives of all whom I meet. Let all the lamps of your people shine as strongly as the stars and the sun.

DAY 25

Arise, shine; for your light has come,
and the glory of the LORD has risen upon you.
For darkness shall cover the earth,
and thick darkness the peoples;
but the LORD will arise upon you,
and his glory will appear over you....
Your sun shall no more go down,
or your moon withdraw itself;
for the LORD will be your everlasting light,
and your days of mourning shall be ended.

ISAIAH 60:1–2, 20

Day of Days

One night there went out over the stillness of the evening breeze, out over those chalky hills of Bethlehem, the cry of a new born babe. "The Word became flesh and dwelt amongst us." Earth did not hear the cry, for the earth slept; men did not hear the cry, for they did not know that a Child could be greater than a man; kings did not hear the cry, for they did not know that a King could be born in a stable; empires did not hear the cry, for empires did not know that an Infant could hold the reins that steer suns and worlds in their courses. But shepherds and philosophers heard the cry, for only the very simple and the very learned know that the heart of a God can cry out in the cry of a Child. And they came with gifts—and adored, and so great was the majesty seated on the brow of the Child, so great was the dignity of the babe, so powerful was the light of these eyes that shone like celestial suns, that they could not help but cry out: "Emmanuel: God is with us."

THE LIFE OF ALL LIVING

❖ ❖ ❖

Let us rejoice now at the reception of our gift of God in human form. Give us ears to hear the cry of the new-born Babe. Come forth with healing to comfort us. As Joseph and Mary were inscribed in the census of the House of David, Lord, let us be inscribed in your heart of hearts, so that as we meet you here at the beginning of your life, we will recognize the shadow of the Cross in the cave at Bethlehem. And when we meet you at the end of your life carrying a cross, we will be humble enough to be found standing beneath it.

DAY 26

Now in Jerusalem by the Sheep Gate there is a pool, called in Hebrew Beth-zatha, which has five porticoes. In these lay many invalids—blind, lame, and paralyzed. One man was there who had been ill for thirty-eight years. When Jesus saw him lying there and knew that he had been there a long time, he said to him, "Do you want to be made well?" The sick man answered him, "Sir, I have no one to put me into the pool when the water is stirred up; and while I am making my way, someone else steps down ahead of me." Jesus said to him, "Stand up, take your mat and walk." At once the man was made well, and he took up his mat and began to walk.

JOHN 5:2–9

Finding God

ost of us are like the man who lay at the Pool of Bethsatha for thirty-eight years who was not cured. His excuse was that when the waters were stirred, there was no one to put him in. He needed healing but he really did not want it. When our Lord appeared, he told the man to do the very thing he thought was impossible, namely, take up his bed. What was wanting was his will. He was moribund because he did not want to be better....

Ever since the days of Adam man has been hiding from God and saying: "God is hard to find." The truth is that in each heart there is a secret garden which God made uniquely for himself. The garden is like a safety deposit vault inasmuch as it has two keys. God has one key, hence the soul cannot let in anyone else but God. The human heart has the other key, hence not even God can get in without man's consent....God is always at that Garden Gate with his key. We pretend to look for ours, saying we cannot find it, but all the while it is in our hand, did we but will to see it. The reason we are not happy is because we do not want God. As Leon Bloy said: "There is only one sadness in life; the sadness of not being a saint."

MODERN SOUL IN SEARCH OF GOD

❖ ❖ ❖

O Sacred Lord, as you draw near to the secret garden of our hearts, dispel the dark shadows of our sins, bring your truth to uplift our ever-weak human natures, and fashion us anew in your image and likeness. Give us the courage to be God-centered souls, to be souls whose wisdom is governed by your Holy Spirit. Give us the grace to be saints.

DAY 27

When the time came for their purification according to the law of Moses, they brought him [Jesus] up to Jerusalem to present him to the Lord (as it is written in the law of the Lord, "Every firstborn male shall be designated as holy to the Lord"), and they offered a sacrifice according to what is stated in the law of the Lord, "a pair of turtledoves or two young pigeons."

Now there was a man in Jerusalem whose name was Simeon; this man was righteous and devout, looking forward to the consolation of Israel, and the Holy Spirit rested on him. It had been revealed to him by the Holy Spirit that he would not see death before he had seen the Lord's Messiah. Guided by the Spirit, Simeon came into the temple; and when the parents brought in the child Jesus, to do for him what was customary under the law, Simeon took him in his arms and praised God, saying,

"Master, now you are dismissing your servant in peace,
according to your word;

for my eyes have seen your salvation,
which you have prepared in the presence of all peoples,
a light for revelation to the Gentiles
and for glory to your people Israel."

LUKE 2:22–32

Flower of the Evening

here are some flowers that open only in the evening; Simeon, the old man, was one of those flowers. Imagine the ecstasy of this old man when he embraced this child, and his first words were, "Now I am ready to die." He then speaks to the mother and notice how he looks backwards and forwards; he looks backward to the people of God of which he was a priest and says, "This is the glory of thy people, Israel, this Babe." Then he looks forward, "This is the Light which shall give revelation to the Gentiles." In other words, he saw in this Babe, the maker of a new covenant, but he also saw in him a sign to be contradicted by the very people to whom he came to bring salvation. So that this Christ who was born was not just someone who came by surprise; he's related to all of the people of God through the centuries.

THE BISHOP SHEEN CATECHISM

✤ ✤ ✤

O God, the expected of all nations, who became a Babe, once more remind us that truth is found in your ways, that injustice cannot be disguised as progress, and freedom does not grant us license. Keep before us the vision of your birth and bring us back to the safety of your care.

DAY 28

"They listened to me, and waited,
and kept silence for my counsel.
After I spoke they did not speak again,
and my word dropped upon them like dew.
They waited for me as for the rain;
they opened their mouths as for the spring rain.
I smiled on them when they had no confidence;
and the light of my countenance
they did not extinguish."

JOB 29:21–24

A Sense of Humor

One night there rang out over the stillness of an evening breeze the cry of the heart of a God in the voice of a child. And when the Babe grew in grace and wisdom, he went into the public lanes and market places, and began to teach a new doctrine to men—the doctrine of the Divine Sense of Humor. Everything he said, everything he did could be summed up in these words: Nothing in this world is to be taken seriously, nothing—except the salvation of a soul.

Such is the history of the Divine Sense of Humor, and now that we know what it is, we may ask who are they who understand and possess it, and here the answer must be that those who possess it in its fullness are saints.

I do not mean canonized saints, but rather that great army of solid Christians to whom everything speaks a story of God's love. A saint can be defined as one who has a Divine Sense of Humor, for a saint never takes the world seriously as the lasting city. To him the world is like a scaffolding up through which souls climb to the Kingdom of Heaven, and when the last soul shall have climbed up through it, then it shall be torn down, not because it is base, but simply because it has done its work.

He who came to this earth to teach us the Divine Sense of Humor showed us everything that was lovely and beautiful in his character—except one thing. He showed us his power; he showed us his wisdom; he showed us his melting kindness; he showed us his sorrow; he showed us his tears; but there was one thing he saved for heaven that will make heaven heaven, and that was—His Smile!

MANIFESTATIONS OF CHRIST

✦ ✦ ✦

In the glow of your birth, O Lord, grant us the joy that sinlessness provides. Keep our love for you alive even as we journey with you to the Cross. Bathe our love in your Divine Sense of Humor—so that we no longer take money seriously, flesh seriously, business seriously, food seriously—but only the state of our souls.

PART II

~~~~~

READINGS *for the* TWELVE DAYS *of* CHRISTMAS

Christmas Day

O come, let us sing to the LORD;
let us make a joyful noise to the
rock of our salvation!
Let us come into his presence with thanksgiving;
let us make a joyful noise to him
with songs of praise!...
O come, let us worship and bow down
let us kneel before the LORD,
our Maker!
For he is our God,
and we are the people of his pasture,
and the sheep of his hand.

PSALM 95:1–7

Alleluia: We Are Redeemed!

"A Child is born." To some He comes on this Christmas Day even in the remorse that follows "There is no room"; to some He comes when their hearts are saddened by a life that has been taken away, and can be gladdened only by a Life that is given; to some He comes when their hearts like conscious mangers cry out "Lord, I am not worthy"; to others He comes as their study of science reminds them that the only star worth studying is the Star that leads to the Maker of the Stars; to others He comes when their hearts are broken, that He might enter in to heal with wings wider than the world; to others He comes in joy amidst the Venite Adoremus of the angels; to others He comes because they are so young they can never remember another Christmas—but to each and everyone He comes as if He had never come before in His own sweet way, He the Child who is born, He…Jesus the Savior, He Emmanuel, He, Christ at Christ's Mass on Christmas—Merry Christmas!!

THE FULLNESS OF CHRIST

✢ ✢ ✢

A Savior has been born to us! Come, let us fix our gaze on the crib and adore Him! Even as we are children of sin and error, living in malice and anger, captive to our self-will, let us become renovated and redeemed by the mercy of the infant who delivers us from the powers of darkness unto the salvation of his great love. O God and Infant, save us! Shepherd us safely home!

DAY 2

"O daughter, you are blessed by the Most High God above all other women on earth; and blessed be the Lord God, who created the heavens and the earth, who has guided you.... Your praise will never depart from the hearts of those who remember the power of God. May God grant this to be a perpetual honor to you, and may he reward you with blessings."

JUDITH 13:18–20

The Paradise of Christmas

*A*s we gather about the crib of Bethlehem, we feel that we are in the presence of a new Paradise of Beauty and Love, ...and the name of that Paradise is Mary. ...And if we could have been there in that stable on that first Christmas night, we might have seen that Paradise of the Incarnation, but we should not be able to recollect whether her face was beautiful or not... for what would have impressed us, and made us forget all else, would have been the lovely, sinless soul that shone through her eyes like two celestial suns....If we could have stood at the gates to that Paradise, we would have less peered at it as into it, for what would have impressed us would not have been any external qualities, though these would have been ravishing, but rather the qualities of her soul—her simplicity, innocence, humility, and above all, her purity....Christmas takes on a new meaning when the Mother is seen with the Babe. In fact, the heavens and the earth seem almost to exchange places. Years ago, we used to think of the heavens as "way up there." Then one day the God of the heavens came to this earth, and that hour when she held the Babe in her arms, it became true to say that with her we now "look down" to heaven.

MANIFESTATIONS OF CHRIST

❖ ❖ ❖

Blessed Mother, let us follow the light of your simplicity and innocence. Guide us in the path of your Son so that we may reflect—however imperfectly—the shining beacon of your love. Let echoes of your goodness follow us all the days of our lives. Let us be faithful to your Son to the end and lead us to our final Paradise where we may rest with you and your Son. Amen.

DAY 3

As God's chosen ones, holy and beloved, clothe yourselves with compassion, kindness, humility, meekness, and patience. Bear with one another and, if anyone has a complaint against another, forgive each other; just as the Lord has forgiven you, so you also must forgive.

COLOSSIANS 3:12–13

No Sin, No Savior

He who refuses to forgive others breaks down the bridge over which he himself must pass, for everyone has need to be forgiven. The Divine Law is that only those who forgive will be forgiven. It is much easier to forgive the weak who have injured us or those who are beneath us in dignity than it is to forgive the powerful or the better or the nobler whom we have injured....In this truth is hidden the explanation of why the Divine who came to bring forgiveness to humans was crucified at the moment of greatest forgiveness. Though the Divine forgiveness comes to those who forgive, nevertheless, some say: "I cannot forgive myself." As Cardinal Newman answered: "No true penitent forgets or forgives himself; an unforgiving spirit towards himself is the very price of God's forgiving him." Of course, no person can forgive himself. He can only be forgiven by Him whom he has injured.

WALK WITH GOD

Blessed Lord and Savior, give us insight to know that the judgments we pronounce on others are most often the judgments that should be applied to ourselves. Remind us under all circumstances that judging others puts our own selves in peril. Let us remember that it is Christ who died for our sins, who forgives each of us, and who is the most merciful.

DAY 4

May the God of peace himself
sanctify you entirely;
and may your spirit
and soul and body
be kept sound and blameless.

1 THESSALONIANS 5:23

False Peace

*J*f Christ is the Prince of Peace...then how do we reconcile these other seemingly contradictory words of Our Lord: "Do not think that I come to send peace upon earth: I came not to send peace, but the sword"; and "Think you, that I am come to give peace on earth? I tell you, no; but separation...."

The explanation of these apparent contradictions is to be found in the words he addressed to his apostles the night of the Last Supper in which he made an important distinction between two kinds of peace: "My peace I give unto you; not as the world gives, do I give unto you"; and "These things I have spoken to you, that in me you may have peace. In the world you shall have distress: but have confidence; I have overcome the world." There is a difference, then, between his Peace and the peace of the world.

It is evident from these words that Our Lord offers a peace and a consolation that he alone can confer, a peace that comes from the right ordering of conscience, from justice, charity, love of God and love of neighbor.

THE CROSS AND THE BEATITUDES

✛ ✛ ✛

Lord of All, give us true interior peace so that we may be called children of God, that we may possess the true peace of a right conscience, not the false peace of injustice and hate; that we may have the true peace of an ordered tranquillity, not the false peace of compromised obedience; that we may embody the true peace of loving our enemies, not the false peace of despising them; that we may possess the true peace of watchful waiting, not the false peace of sleeping during the appointed hours.

DAY 5

Now to God who is able to strengthen you according to my gospel and the proclamation of Jesus Christ, according to the revelation of the mystery that was kept secret for long ages but is now disclosed, and through the prophetic writings is made known to all the Gentiles, according to the command of the eternal God, to bring about the obedience of faith—to the only wise God, through Jesus Christ, to whom be the glory forever! Amen.

ROMANS 16:25–27

Faith and Obedience

What does obedience do for us? Obedience gives us faith....Are we reacting against Christ and his Church, or are we accepting its authority? Faith comes from that kind of submission. Remember that when our blessed Lord was born, Herod consulted the scribes....He said to the scribes, "Where is Christ to be born?"...They said, "He is to be born in Bethlehem." Did they go? There was not a single scribe at the crib—not one. But they knew. Our faith today can be a kind of creedal assent, instead of a living act of the will, conscious of the fact that we are submitting to Christ, as Christ submitted to the heavenly Father....Notice, too, that at the crib, only two classes of people found their way to Christ when he came to this earth: the very simple, and the very learned—the shepherds who knew that they knew nothing, and the wise men who knew that they did not know everything.

THROUGH THE YEAR WITH FULTON SHEEN

Let us listen with open ears and hearts, O Lord, to your words as recorded in Matthew: "All authority in heaven and earth have been given to me." Let us truly acknowledge and meditate on the whole truth of these words, even as the search for power over the earth and over others has become a hallmark of a modern society seemingly bent on self-aggrandizement. Let us wear our faith, then, as the sign of a true pilgrim whose journey is to union in glory with God hereafter.

DAY 6

Brothers and sisters, we are debtors, not to the flesh, to live according to the flesh—for if you live according to the flesh, you will die; but if by the Spirit you put to death the deeds of the body, you will live.

ROMANS 8:12–13

Happiness and Self-Denial

*H*appiness does not come to those who want to know all, or to possess all, or to enjoy all; rather it comes to those who set limitations upon the satisfaction of self. A man, for example, cannot get the whole world into his hands, but he can wash himself of the world. Our powers of dispossession are greater than our powers of possession; there is a limit to what we can gain, but there is no limit to what we can renounce. In the end, the man who wants nothing is the man who has everything, for there is nothing that he desires....

To deny self is to refuse indulgence to lower desires, to put a restraint upon ourselves, to act differently from the way the sensual in our nature would lead us. Self-denial is the test of love, whether it be human or divine....There may be pain in self-denial for a moment, but pain in the pursuit of the highest is certainly more joyful than ease in the neglect of duty. The agony in self-denial is momentary, but the joy that flows from it is lasting.

THE POWER OF LOVE

❖ ❖ ❖

Blessed Lord, give me the spirit of nonpossession and self-denial. Make the doing of your Word paramount over the pursuit of ease. Keep me from throwing myself at every fancy paraded before me, and help me to forego the desire to taste and touch the wonders of this world, lest, blinded by my own self-preoccupation, I lose the glories of the next.

DAY 7

After these things, Joseph of Arimathea, who was a disciple of Jesus, though a secret one because of his fear of the Jews, asked Pilate to let him take away the body of Jesus. Pilate gave him permission; so he came and removed his body. Nicodemus, who had at first come to Jesus by night, also came, bringing a mixture of myrrh and aloes, weighing about a hundred pounds. They took the body of Jesus and wrapped it with the spices in linen clothes, according to the burial custom of the Jews.

JOHN 19:38–40

Gifts of the Magi

*T*he Magi came from the East. How did they know about Christ? Probably from the prophecy of Daniel concerning the seventy weeks of the years; they counted the revolution of the stars. In any case, they knew, and they brought gold because he was a king, incense because he was a priest, but also myrrh. That's the way he was buried, with a hundred pounds of spices and myrrh. What would our mothers have thought if the neighbors brought in embalming fluid when we were born?

THROUGH THE YEAR WITH FULTON SHEEN

In the spirit of the prophet Daniel, let us pray: O Lord, great and steadfast, let your anger and wrath at our sins be turned away from us—even though we are a disgrace among all. Take pity on our desolation. We do not present our request to you because of our repentance, but on the grounds of your great mercy. Hear, O Lord, and forgive us. Do not delay your help.

DAY 8

"Very truly, I tell you, you will weep and mourn, but the world will rejoice; you will have pain, but your pain will turn into joy. When a woman is in labor, she has pain, because her hour has come. But when her child is born, she no longer remembers the anguish because of the joy of having brought a human being into the world. So you have pain now; but I will see you again, and your hearts will rejoice, and no one will take your joy from you."

JOHN 16:20–22

Joyful Redemption

*T*he joy born of love of God enables us to see the world from an entirely different point of view. Before, when shackled to the ego, we were cooped up within the narrow walls of space and time. But once the chains are broken, one falls heir to immensities beyond all telling. Then we find our greatest joys not in the things we cling to, but in what we surrender; not in the asking for anything, but in the giving of something; not in what others can do for us, but in what we can do for others. Joy comes from using well the talents the Lord gave us, from a sense of being redeemed by Our Lord.

GUIDE TO CONTENTMENT

✤ ✤ ✤

May our hearts be so joyful that we desire to share the Good News of your son with our brothers and sisters so that they, too, will know the peace you give to those invited to your redemption. Let our faith be expansive and not exclusive, in Jesus Christ, Our Lord. Amen.

DAY 9

[T]he one who sows sparingly will also reap sparingly, and the one who sows bountifully will also reap bountifully. Each of you must give as you have made up your mind, not reluctantly or under compulsion, for God loves a cheerful giver.

2 CORINTHIANS 9:6–7

The Sanctity of Cheerfulness

*T*he cheerful person always sees in any present evil some prospective good; in pain he sees a Cross from which will issue a Resurrection; in trial, he finds correction and discipline and an opportunity to grow in wisdom; in sorrow, he gathers patience and resignation to the Will of God.

Helping others is not only the cause of cheerfulness, but also the fuel which keeps it burning. As Helen Keller, seeing through blindness, wrote, "Join the great company of those who make the barren places of life fruitful with kindness. The great enduring realities are love and service. Joy is the only fire that keeps our purpose warm and our intelligence aglow."

GUIDE TO CONTENTMENT

O God, let my heart be a cheerful home for your arrival this Christmas season and let the Incarnation take firmly hold there so I may wear joyfulness as an invincible armor against all difficulties.

[O]bey your earthly masters with fear and trembling, in singleness of heart, as you obey Christ; not only while being watched, and in order to please them, but as slaves of Christ, doing the will of God from the heart. Render service with enthusiasm, as to the Lord and not to men and women, knowing that whatever good we do, we will receive the same again from the Lord.

EPHESIANS 6:5–8

Divine Enthusiasm

J t is not to be thought that life is a snare or an illusion because
the bubbles cease in a champagne glass. No true unhappiness comes to human beings unless they place their hearts in
a false infinite. Those who see that all human life is nothing but
Divine Love on pilgrimage will use it as a kind of Jacob's ladder to climb back again through virtue to the source of all love
which is God himself. Such spiritual fires never cool, because
they are not fed by glands, but glow with the coals lighted at the
furnace of heaven….To be enthusiastic in that case is to live out
the meaning of the word, for enthusiasm comes from two Greek
words meaning "to be in God."

LIFE IS WORTH LIVING (1ST SERIES)

O Lord, during this season of great anticipation, give us
strength to regain our step on the ladder of virtue. Let our
enthusiasm be fanned, not by false love or by immediate
sensory gratification but by the spiritual love that comes
only after proper waiting. Give us the grace of stillness,
not the temporary effervescence of earthly bubbles that
burst and flatten with the fizz of selfishness.

DAY 11

Now every year his parents went to Jerusalem for the festival of the Passover. And when he [Jesus] was twelve years old, they went up as usual for the festival. When the festival was ended and they started to return, the boy Jesus stayed behind in Jerusalem, but his parents did not know it. Assuming that he was in the group of travelers, they went a day's journey. Then they started to look for him among their relatives and friends. When they did not find him, they returned to Jerusalem to search for him. After three days they found him in the temple, sitting among the teachers, listening to them and asking them questions. And all who heard him were amazed at his understanding and his answers. When his parents saw him they were astonished; and his mother said to him, "Child, why have you treated us like this? Look, your father and I have been searching for you in great anxiety." He said to them, "Why were you searching for me? Did you not know that I must be in my Father's house?" But they did not understand what he said to them.

Then he went down with them and came to Nazareth, and was obedient to them.

LUKE 2:41–51

Bedrock Obedience

hat a beautiful lesson of obedience is given to us in the divine Child of Nazareth. There is no evidence that He ever gave to Mary and Joseph just the nominal right to command, rather, the Scripture says He lived there in subjection to them. Imagine, God subject to man—God, before whom the angels and principalities tremble, is subject to Mary and to Joseph. Here are two great miracles of humility and exaltation: the God-man obeying a woman, and a woman commanding the God-man, and that obedience lasted for thirty years. By this long span of voluntary obedience, He revealed that the Fourth Commandment is the bedrock of family life. In a larger way, how else could the primal sin of disobedience against God be undone except by the obedience in the flesh of the very God who was once defied. It was Lucifer who said, "I will not obey," and Eden caught up that echo.

THE BISHOP SHEEN CATECHISM

❖ ❖ ❖

By your example given so dutifully during your hidden childhood in Nazareth, show us the value of harmony and obedience in all our relationships. Let us not be captive to popular but misguided notions of community and family, but liberate us so that we may speak words of love and in this way let us grow in wisdom and grace. Join us together so that we may unleash goodness and be the "living rock" of the fullness of faith.

DAY 12

Grace to you and peace
from God our Father
and the Lord Jesus Christ,
who gave himself for our sins
to set us free from the present evil age,
according to the will
of our God and Father,
to whom be the glory
forever and ever.

GALATIANS 1:3–5

Christmas Peace

All love craves a cross—even God's. True love is sacrificial. That is why courtship is characterized by gift-giving—a surrender of what one has. In marriage this sacrificial love should deepen by a surrender of what one has. Because too many measure their love for one another by the pleasure which the other gives, they are in reality not in love, but in the swamps of selfishness.... Our poor, frail human souls at best are like jangled strings, made toneless by self-love; and not until we tighten them with self-discipline can we attune them to those harmonies that come from God, wherein each, having given to the other hostage of its heart, finds himself free in the glorious liberty of the children of God.

Peace first came to the world when the Wise Men discovered a family. And the dawn of peace will come again when other wise men return to homes where they see the human family of father, mother, and children, as the reverse order of the Holy Family: a Child, a Mother, and a Father.

SEVEN PILLARS OF PEACE

✦ ✦ ✦

Let "Alleluia! Christ is born to set us free" be our song of joy. May we work to achieve this authentic freedom which is grounded in the truth and peace of Jesus Christ. May Christ shine through our eyes, work through our hands, and speak through our lips, so that true peace will surround us and violence and discord be banished in the overwhelming force of God's love. May we learn to measure our love by how much we give and not by how much we receive. May our families prosper in true imitation of that most holy of families.

PART III

~~~~~~~

A FORMAT for
EVENING
PRAYER

Format for Nightly Prayer and Reading

THE PURPOSE of presenting these two optional formats for nightly readings and prayer is to offer a way to use the material in this book as an opportunity for group or individual prayer. Of course, there are other ways in which to use this material, for example, as a vehicle for meditation or as promptings for completing a prayer journal.

FORMAT 1

OPENING PRAYER

The observance begins with these words:

God, come to my assistance.
Lord, make haste to help me.

followed by:

Glory to the Father and to the Son,
and to the Holy Spirit: as it was in the beginning, is now,
and will be for ever. Amen. Alleluia.

EXAMINATION OF CONSCIENCE

If this observance is being prayed individually, an examination of conscience may be included. Here is a short examination of conscience; you may, of course, use your own preferred method.

1. Place yourself in a quiet frame of mind.
2. Review your life since your last confession.
3. Reflect on the Ten Commandments and any sins against these commandments.
4. Reflect on the words of the gospel, especially Jesus' commandment to love your neighbor as yourself.
5. Ask yourself these questions: How have I been unkind—in thoughts, words, and actions? Am I refusing to forgive anyone? Do I despise any group or person? Am I a prisoner of fear, anxiety, worry, guilt, inferiority, or hatred of myself?

PENITENTIAL RITE (OPTIONAL)

If a group of people are praying in unison, a penitential rite from *The Roman Missal* may be used:

Presider: Lord Jesus, you came to call all people to yourself: Lord, have mercy.

All: Lord, have mercy.

Presider: Lord Jesus, you come to us in word and prayer: Christ, have mercy.

All: Christ, have mercy.

Presider: Lord Jesus, you will appear in glory with all your saints: Lord, have mercy.

All: Lord, have mercy.

Presider: May almighty God have mercy on us, forgive us our sins, and bring us to life everlasting.

All: Amen.

HYMN: O COME, O COME, EMMANUEL

A hymn is now sung or recited. This Advent hymn is a paraphrase of the "Great O" Antiphons written in the twelfth century and translated by John Mason Neale in 1852.

O come, O come, Emmanuel,
And ransom captive Israel;
That mourns in lonely exile here,
Until the Son of God appear.

Refrain: Rejoice! Rejoice! O Israel
          To thee shall come, Emmanuel!

O come, thou wisdom, from on high,
And order all things far and nigh;
To us the path of knowledge show,
And teach us in her ways to go.

Refrain

O come, O come, thou Lord of might,
Who to thy tribes on Sinai's height
In ancient times did give the law,
In cloud, and majesty, and awe.

Refrain

O come, thou rod of Jesse's stem,
From ev'ry foe deliver them
That trust thy mighty power to save,
And give them vict'ry o'er the grave.

Refrain

O come, thou key of David come,
And open wide our heav'nly home,
Make safe the way that leads on high,
That we no more have cause to sigh.

Refrain

O come, thou Dayspring from on high,
And cheer us by thy drawing nigh;
Disperse the gloomy clouds of night
And death's dark shadow put to flight.

Refrain

O come, Desire of nations, bind
In one the hearts of all mankind;
Bid every strife and quarrel cease
And fill the world with heaven's peace.

Refrain

PSALM 27:7–14—GOD STANDS BY US IN DANGERS

Hear, O LORD, when I cry aloud,
    be gracious to me and answer me!
"Come," my heart says, "seek his face!"
    Your face, LORD, do I seek.
    Do not hide your face from me.

Do not turn your servant away in anger,
    you who have been my help.
Do not cast me off, do not forsake me,...
    the LORD will take me up.

Teach me your way, O LORD,
  and lead me on a level path
  because of my enemies.
Do not give me up to the will of my adversaries,
  for false witnesses have risen against me,
  and they are breathing out violence.

I believe that I shall see the goodness of the LORD
  in the land of the living.
Wait for the LORD;
  be strong, and let your heart take courage;
  wait for the LORD.

RESPONSE

I long to see your face, O Lord. You are my light and my help. Do
not turn away from me.

SCRIPTURE READING

Read silently or have a presider proclaim the Scripture of the day
that is selected.

RESPONSE

Come and set us free, Lord God of power and might. Let your
face shine on us and we will be saved.

Glory to the Father and to the Son,
and to the Holy Spirit: as it was in the beginning, is now,
and will be for ever. Amen. Alleluia.

SECOND READING

Read the excerpt from Bishop Sheen for the day selected.

CANTICLE OF SIMEON

Lord, now you let your servant go in peace;
your word has been fulfilled:
my own eyes have seen the salvation
which you have prepared in the sight of every people:
a light to reveal you to the nations
and the glory of your people Israel.
Glory to the Father, and to the Son, and to the Holy Spirit:
as it was in the beginning, is now, and will be for ever. Amen.

PRAYER

Say the prayer following the selected excerpt from Bishop Sheen.

BLESSING

May the Lord grant us a restful night and a peaceful death. Amen.

MARIAN ANTIPHON

Loving mother of the Redeemer,
gate of heaven, star of the sea,
assist your people who have fallen yet strive to rise again.
To the wonderment of nature you bore your Creator,
yet remained a virgin after as before.
You who received Gabriel's joyful greeting,
have pity on us poor sinners.

FORMAT 2

OPENING PRAYER

The observance begins with these words:

> *God, come to my assistance.*
> *Lord, make haste to help me.*

followed by:

> *Glory to the Father and to the Son,*
> *and to the Holy Spirit: as it was in the beginning, is now,*
> *and will be for ever. Amen. Alleluia.*

EXAMINATION OF CONSCIENCE

If this observance is being prayed individually, an examination of conscience may be included. Here is a short examination of conscience; you may, of course, use your own preferred method.

1. Place yourself in a quiet frame of mind.
2. Review your life since your last confession.
3. Reflect on the Ten Commandments and any sins against these commandments.
4. Reflect on the words of the gospel, especially Jesus' commandment to love your neighbor as yourself.
5. Ask yourself these questions: How have I been unkind—in thoughts, words, and actions? Am I refusing to forgive anyone? Do I despise any group or person? Am I a prisoner of fear, anxiety, worry, guilt, inferiority, or hatred of myself?

PENITENTIAL RITE (OPTIONAL)

If a group of people are praying in unison, a penitential rite from *The Roman Missal* may be used:

All: I confess to almighty God,
and to you, my brothers and sisters,
that I have greatly sinned
in my thoughts and in my words,
in what I have done,
and in what I have failed to do;
through my fault,
through my fault,
through my most grievous fault;
therefore I ask blessed Mary, ever-Virgin,
all the angels and saints,
and you, my brothers and sisters,
to pray for me to the Lord our God.

Presider: May almighty God have mercy on us, forgive us our sins, and bring us to life everlasting.

All: Amen.

Hymn: Behold, a Rose

A hymn is now sung or recited. This traditional hymn was composed in German in the fifteenth century. It is sung to the melody of the familiar "Lo, A Rose E're Blooming."

Behold, a rose of Judah
From tender branch has sprung,
From Jesse's lineage coming,
As men of old have sung.
It came a flower bright
Amid the cold of winter,
When half spent was the night.

Isaiah has foretold it
In words of promise sure,
And Mary's arms enfolt it,
A virgin meek and pure.
Through God's eternal will
She bore for men a savior
At midnight calm and still.

Psalm 40:1–8—Thanksgiving for Deliverance

I waited patiently for the LORD;
    he inclined to me and heard my cry.
He drew me up from the desolate pit,
    out of the miry bog,
and set my feet upon a rock,
    making my steps secure.
He put a new song in my mouth,
    a song of praise to our God.
Many will see and fear,
    and put their trust in the LORD.

Happy are those who make
     the LORD their trust,
who do not turn to the proud,
     to those who go astray after false gods.
You have multiplied, O LORD my God,
     your wondrous deeds and your thoughts towards us;
     none can compare with you.
Were I to proclaim and tell of them,
     they would be more than can be counted.

Sacrifice and offering you do not desire,
     but you have given me an open ear.
Burnt-offering and sin-offering
     you have not required.
Then I said, "Here I am;
     in the scroll of the book it is written of me.
I delight to do your will, O my God;
     your law is within my heart."

RESPONSE

May all who seek after you be glad in the Lord, may those who
find your salvation say with continuous praise "Great is the Lord!"

SCRIPTURE READING

Read silently or have a presider proclaim the Scripture of the day
that is selected.

RESPONSE

Lord, you who were made obedient unto death, teach us to always do the Father's will, so that, sanctified by the holy obedience that joins us to your sacrifice, we can count on your immense love in times of sorrow.

Glory be to the Father, and to the Son,
and to the Holy Spirit: as it was in the beginning, is now,
and will be for ever. Amen. Alleluia.

SECOND READING

Read silently or have a presider read the words of Bishop Sheen for the day selected.

CANTICLE OF SIMEON

Lord, now you let your servant go in peace;
your word has been fulfilled:
my own eyes have seen the salvation
which you have prepared in the sight of every people:
a light to reveal you to the nations
and the glory of your people Israel.
Glory to the Father, and to the Son,
and to the Holy Spirit:
as it was in the beginning, is now,
and will be for ever. Amen.

PRAYER

Recite the prayer that follows the excerpt from Bishop Sheen for the day selected.

BLESSING

Lord, give our bodies restful sleep and let the work we have done today bear fruit in eternal life. Watch over us as we rest in your peace. Amen.

MARIAN ANTIPHON

Hail, holy Queen, mother of mercy,
    our life, our sweetness, and our hope.
To you do we cry,
    poor banished children of Eve.
To you do we send up our sighs,
    mourning and weeping in this vale of tears.
Turn then, most gracious advocate,
    your eyes of mercy toward us,
    and after this exile
    show to us the blessed fruit of your womb, Jesus.
O clement, O loving,
O sweet Virgin Mary.

Sources and Acknowledgments

The Bishop Sheen Catechism: A Catholic Encyclopedia. Germansville, Penn.: Jon R. Hallingstad, 1986.

Cross and the Beatitudes: Lessons on Love and Forgiveness. Liguori, Mo.: Liguori/Triumph, 2000.

The Eternal Galilean. New York: Appleton-Century, 1934.

The Fullness of Christ, Published by the National Council of Catholic Men, from nineteen addresses delivered in the Catholic Hour, produced by the National Council of Catholic Men, with the co-operation of the National Broadcasting Company, n.d.

Fulton J. Sheen's Guide to Contentment. New York: Simon and Schuster, 1967.

Go to Heaven. New York: McGraw-Hill Book Company, 1960.

God Love You. New York: Garden City Books, 1955.

In the Fullness of Time: Christ-Centered Wisdom for the Third Millennium. Liguori, Mo.: Liguori/Triumph, 1999.

Life Is Worth Living. First Series. Garden City, N.Y.: Garden City Books, 1953.

The Life of All Living. New York: Century Co., 1929.

Life of Christ. New York: McGraw-Hill Book Company, 1958.

Lift Up Your Heart: A Guide to Spiritual Peace. Liguori, Mo.: Liguori/Triumph, 1996. Previously published by McGraw-Hill, 1950.

Manifestations of Christ. Thirteen addresses delivered in the Catholic Hour, sponsored by the National Council of Catholic Men with the co-operation of the National Broadcasting Company, n.d.

Modern Soul in Search of God. Thirteen addresses delivered in the nation-wide Catholic Hour, produced by the National Council of Catholic Men, in cooperation with the National Broadcasting Company, n.d.

Moods and Truths. New York: The Century Co. (A Popular Library Edition), 1932.

On Being Human: Reflections on Life and Living. Garden City, N.Y.: Doubleday, 1982.

Peace of Soul: Timeless Wisdom on Finding Serenity and Joy. Liguori, Mo.: Liguori/Triumph, 1996. Previously published by McGraw-Hill, 1949.

The power of Love. New York: Maco Corporation, Inc., 1964.

Preface to Religion. New York: P. J. Kenedy & Sons, 1946.

Rejoice: Experiencing the Joy of Christmas Each Day of the Year. Garden City, N.Y.: Image Books (A Division of Doubleday & Company, Inc.), 1984. Previously published as *Christmas Inspirations.*

Seven Pillars of Peace. New York: Charles Scribner's Sons, New York, 1944.

Seven Words of Jesus and Mary. Liguori, Mo.: Liguori/Triumph, 2000. Previously published by P. J. Kenedy & Sons.

Simple Truths: Thinking Life Through With Fulton J. Sheen. Liguori, Mo.: Liguori/Triumph, 1998.

Through the Year With Fulton Sheen. Compiled and edited by Henry Dieterich. New York: Phoenix Press, 1985, 1987.

Walk With God. New York: Maco Magazine Corporation, 757 Third Ave., New York, N.Y. 10017, 1965.

Way to Inner Peace. Garden City, N.Y.: Garden City Books, 1955.

The World's First Love: A Moving and Eloquent Portrayal of Mary, Mother of God. Garden City, N.Y.: Image Books (a division of Doubleday & Company, Inc.), 1956. Previously published by McGraw-Hill Book Company, Inc., 1952.

CPSIA information can be obtained
at www.ICGtesting.com
Printed in the USA
BVHW01s2248051217
502081BV00001B/15/P